CROSS STITCH
HERBS, FRUIT
& FLOWERS

Sophie Hélène

Photographs: Julien Clapot (pages 28, 42 and 54)

Pierre Ferbos (page 18)

Design: Audrey Kerdoncuff (pages 28, 42 and 54)

Charlotte Vannier (page 18)

SEARCH PRESS

introduction

Cross stitch is one of the easiest stitches and can be embroidered on any fabric with any type of thread. All you need to know is how to count and how to follow cross stitch patterns!

From dog rose, sage, bay, poppy and daisy to St John's wort – each double page spread of this book shows patterns for different plants, which can be embroidered separately or together to form delightful cross stitch designs.

This book, packed full of ideas, is the ideal starting point for designing and making your own cross stitch creations.

Both novice and experienced stitchers can use this book as a source of ideas: flick through, dip in, mix them up, change the colours, use different fabrics and compose new designs for decorating clothes, bags, tablecloths, napkins – in fact, any item that is made of fabric can be enhanced by the addition of a simple embroidered design.

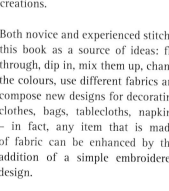

Aromatic plants

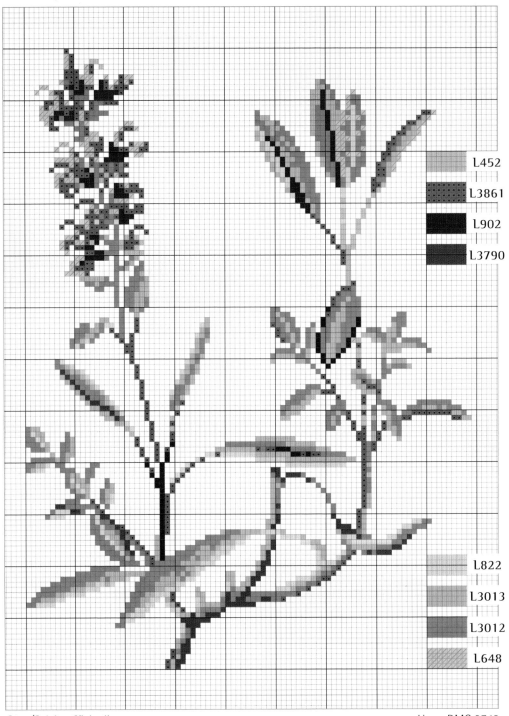

L452
L3861
L902
L3790

L822
L3013
L3012
L648

Sage/Salvia officinalis

Linen DMC 3743

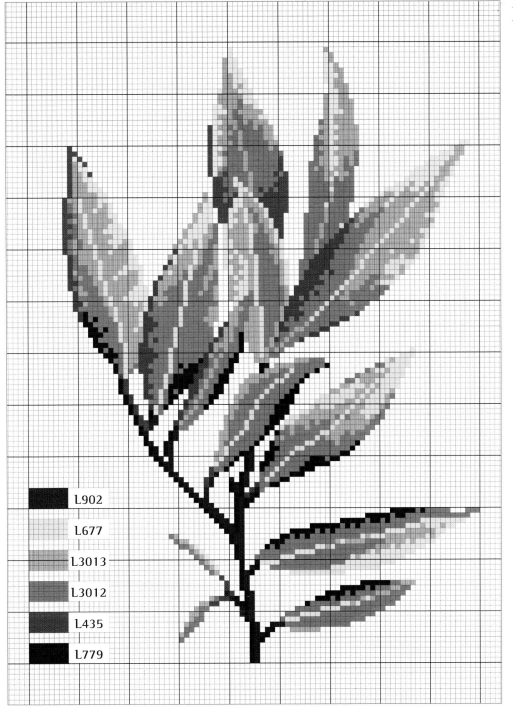

Bay/Laurus nobilis

Linen DMC 712

Legend:
- L902
- L677
- L3013
- L3012
- L435
- L779

Aromatic plants

L677
L833
L3013
L3012
L3790
L648

Fennel/Foeniculum vulgare

Linen DMC 842

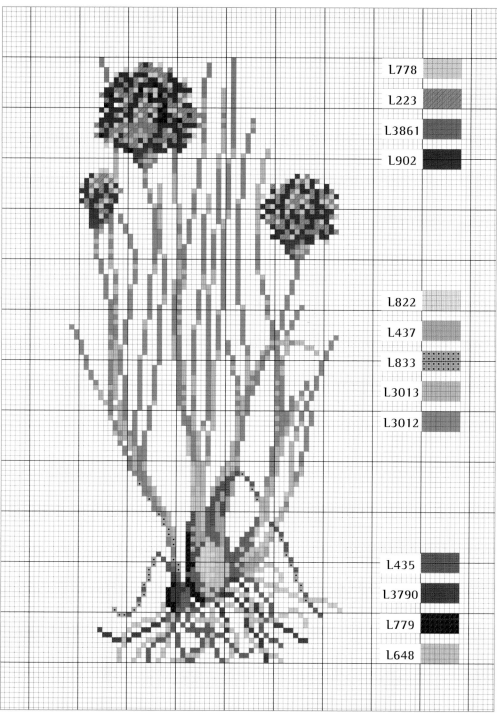

L778
L223
L3861
L902

L822
L437
L833
L3013
L3012

L435
L3790
L779
L648

Chives/Allium schoenoprasum

Linen DMC 3865

Aromatic plants

Legend:
- L677
- L833
- L3013
- L3012
- L435

Dill/Anethum graveolens

Linen DMC 842

	L225
	L778
	L3861
	L677
	L3013
	L3012
	L3790
	L779

Mint/Mentha suaveolens

Linen DMC 3743

Wild salad

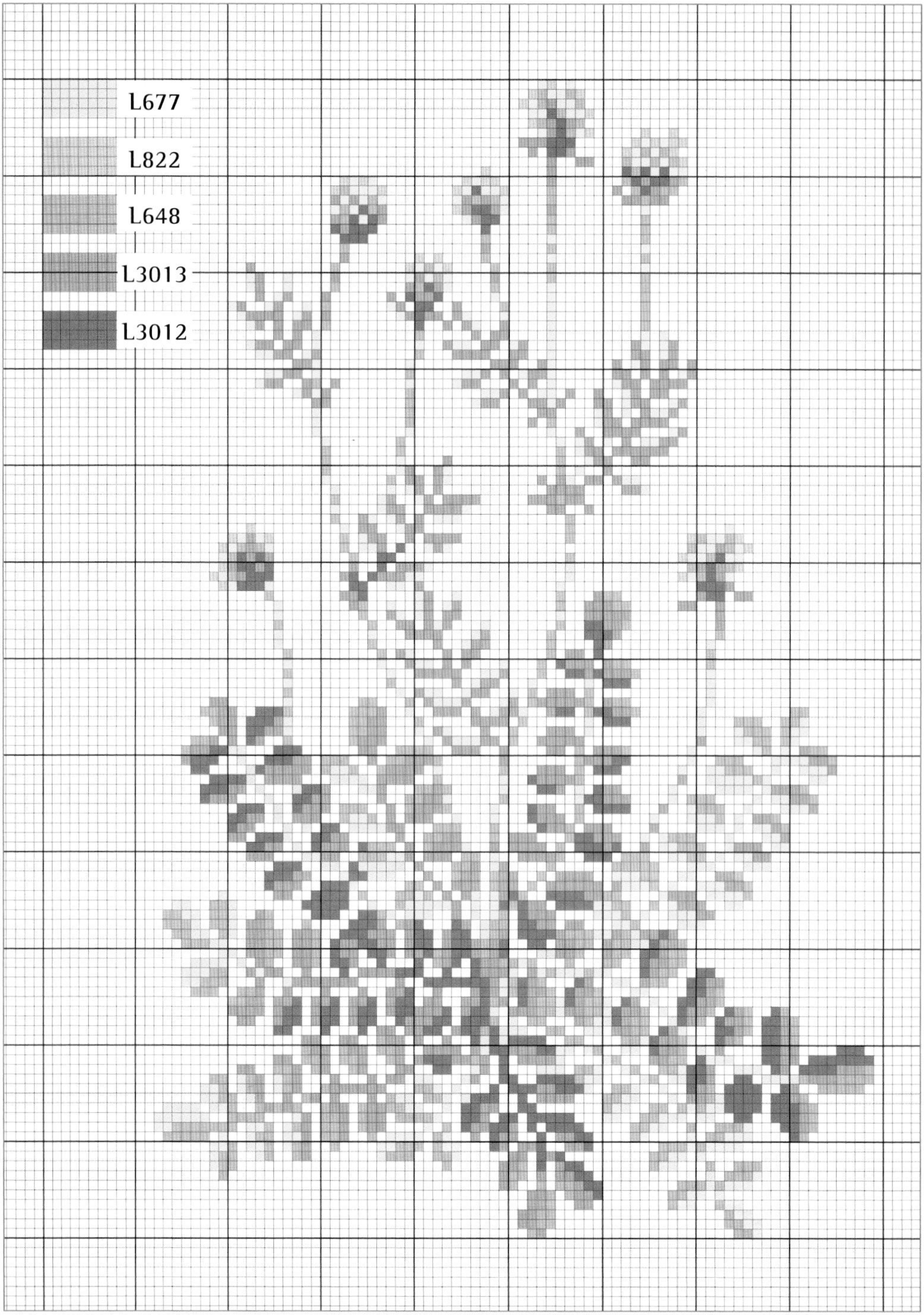

- L677
- L822
- L648
- L3013
- L3012

Salad burnet/Sanguisorba minor Scop.

Linen DMC 3782

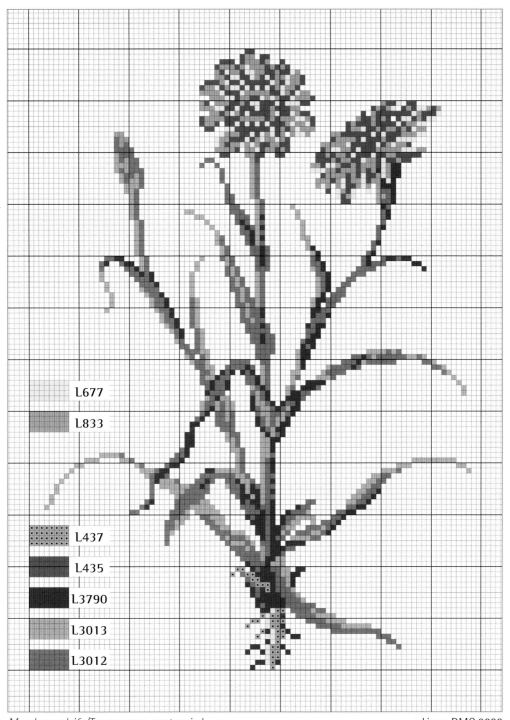

L677

L833

L437

L435

L3790

L3013

L3012

Meadow salsify/Tragopogon pratensis L.

Linen DMC 3823

Wild salad

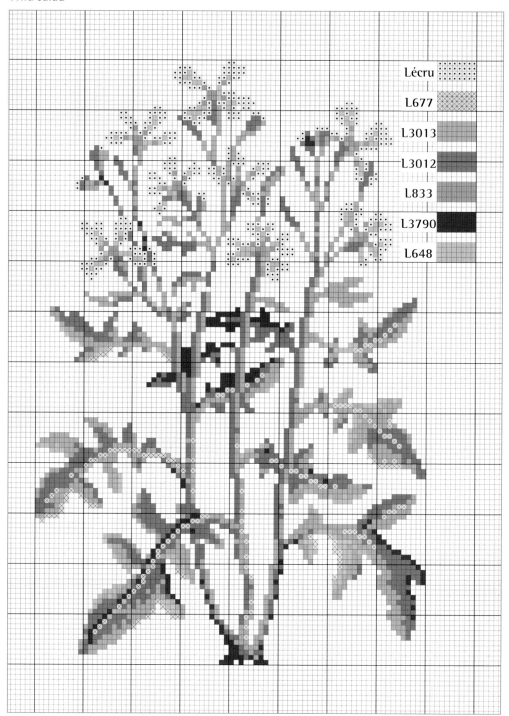

Lécru

L677

L3013

L3012

L833

L3790

L648

Rocket/Eruca sativa

Linen DMC 3782

Legend:
- L677
- L3013
- L3012
- L435
- L3790
- L779
- L3790
- L648

Shepherd's purse/Capsella bursa-pastoris

Linen DMC 842

Wild salad

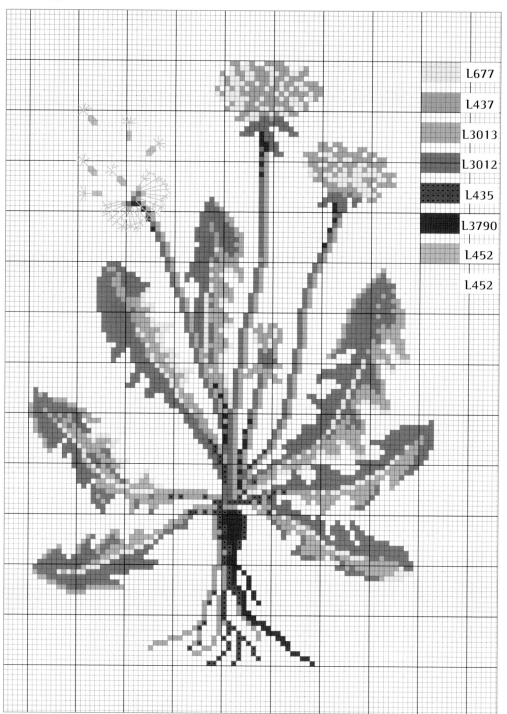

L677
L437
L3013
L3012
L435
L3790
L452
L452

Dandelion/Taraxacum officinale

Linen DMC 842

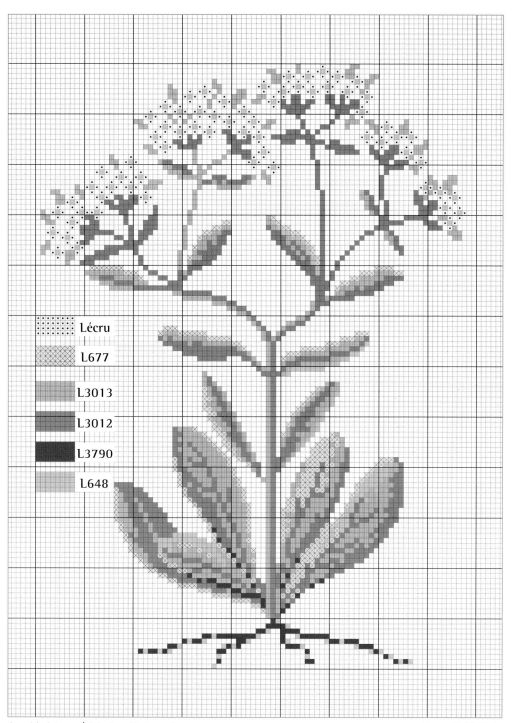

Légende:
- Lécru
- L677
- L3013
- L3012
- L3790
- L648

Lamb's lettuce/Valerianella locusta

Linen DMC 3743

Little fruits of the forest

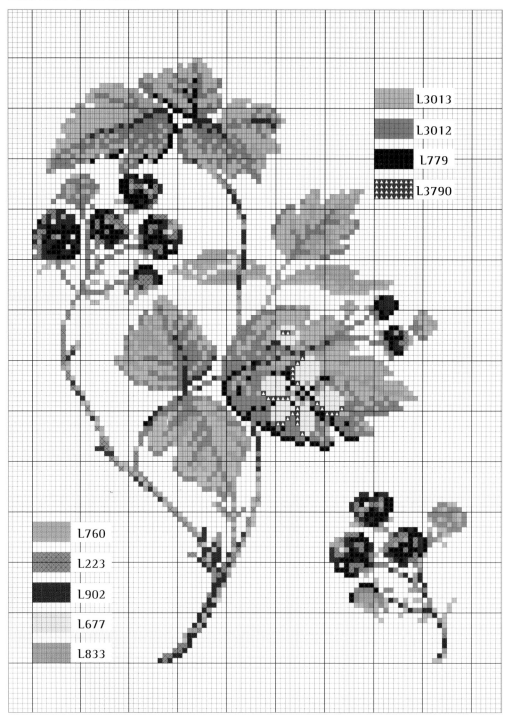

L3013

L3012

L779

L3790

L760

L223

L902

L677

L833

Bramble bush/Rubus fruticosus   Linen DMC 3865

L760
L223
L902

L677
L3790
L3013
L3012

Raspberry bush/Rubus idaeus   Linen DMC 3865

Little fruits of the forest

	L822
	L3861
	L162
	L159
	L3013
	L3012
	L3790
	L779

Sloe/Prunus spinosa

Linen DMC 739

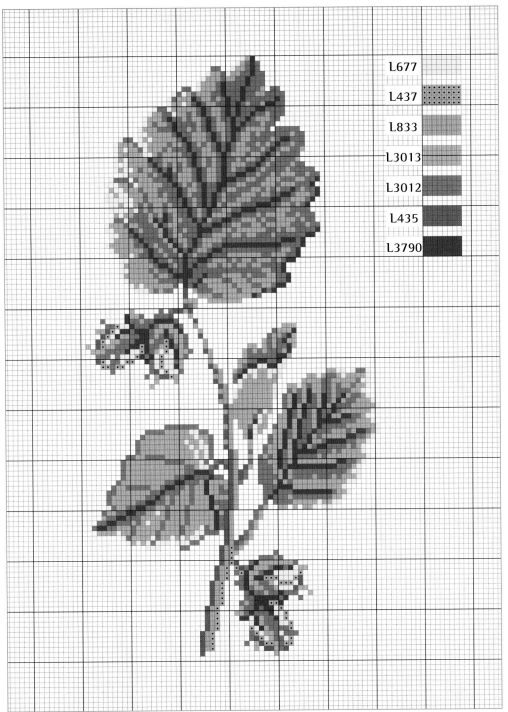

L677
L437
L833
L3013
L3012
L435
L3790

Hazel/Corylus avellana L.

Linen DMC 712

Edible forest plants

L223
L902
L437
L3013
L3012
L3790
L648
L902

Hawthorn/Crataegus oxyacantha L.

Linen DMC 3743

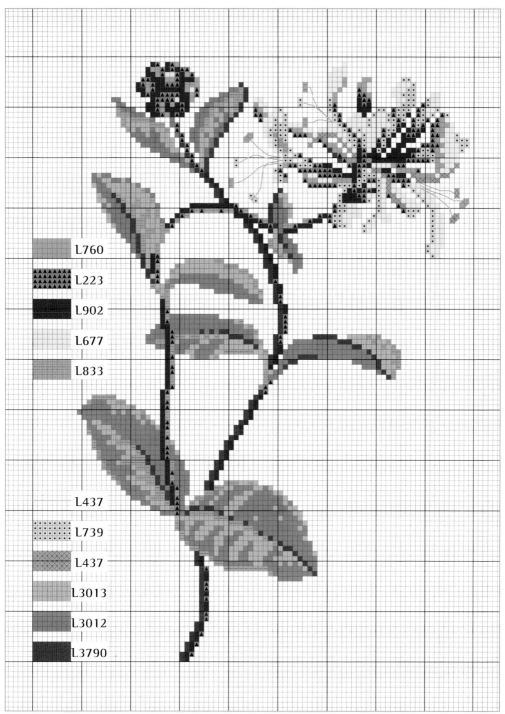

L760
L223
L902
L677
L833

L437
L739
L437
L3013
L3012
L3790

Honeysuckle/Lonicera periclymenum

Linen DMC 772

Edible forest plants

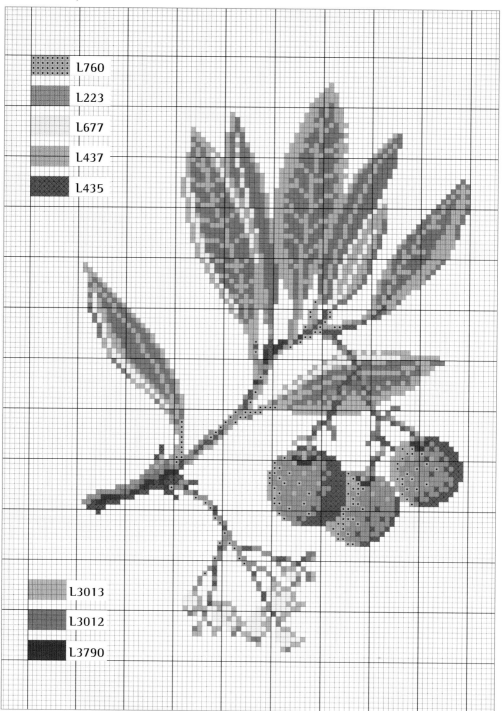

	L760
	L223
	L677
	L437
	L435
	L3013
	L3012
	L3790

Strawberry tree/Arbutus unedo L.

Linen DMC 225

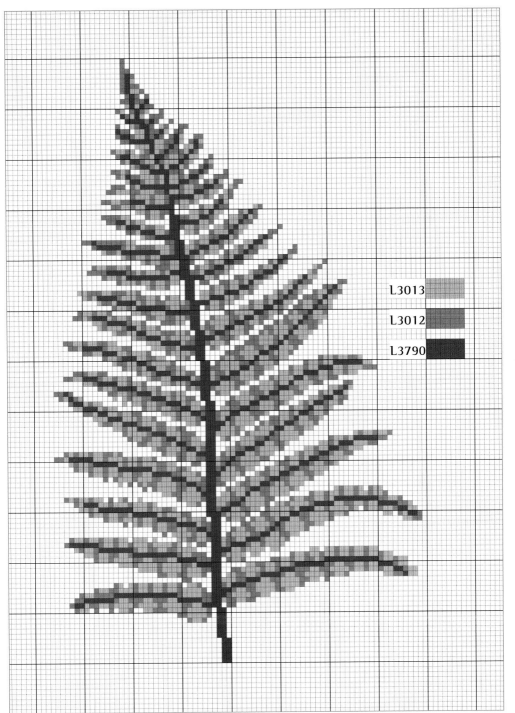

L3013

L3012

L3790

Male fern/Dryopteris filix-mas (L.) schott

Linen DMC 842

Medicinal plants

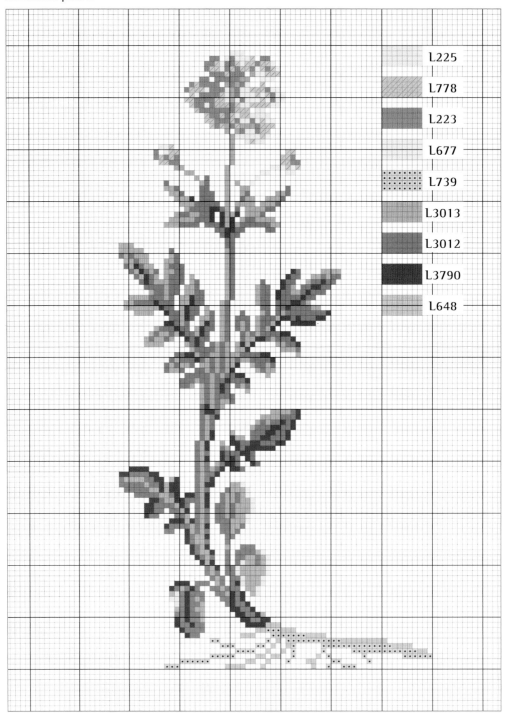

L225
L778
L223
L677
L739
L3013
L3012
L3790
L648

Valerian/Valeriana officinalis L.

Linen DMC 3865

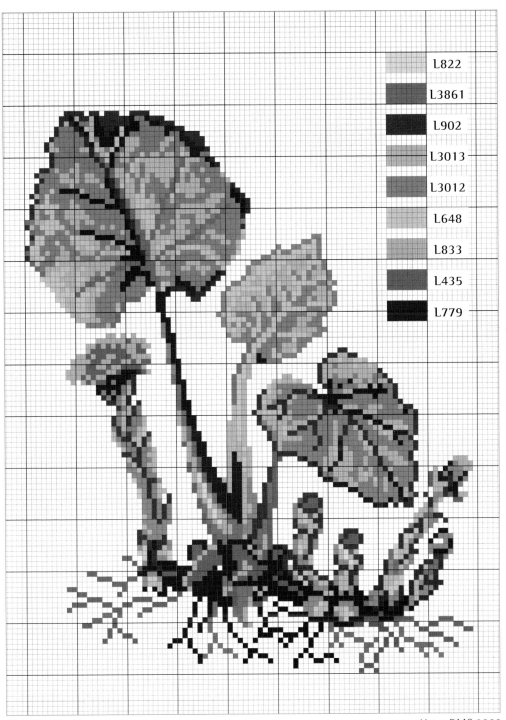

	L822
	L3861
	L902
	L3013
	L3012
	L648
	L833
	L435
	L779

Coltsfoot/Tussilago farfara L.

Linen DMC 3866

Medicinal plants

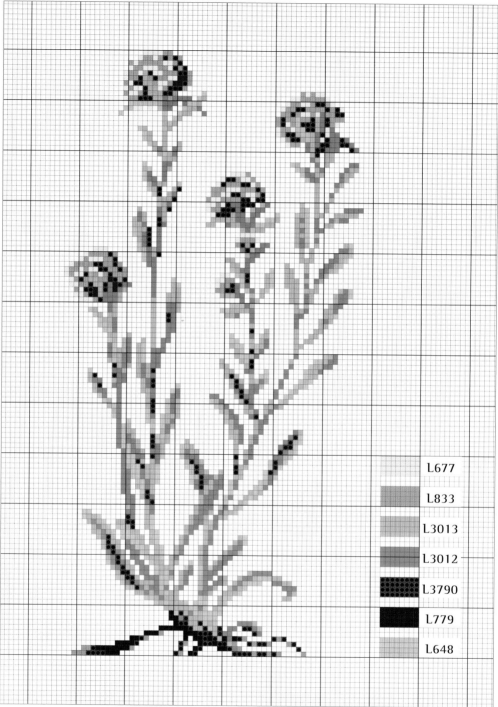

Legend:
- L677
- L833
- L3013
- L3012
- L3790
- L779
- L648

Dwarf everlast/Helichrysum arenarium

Linen DMC 842

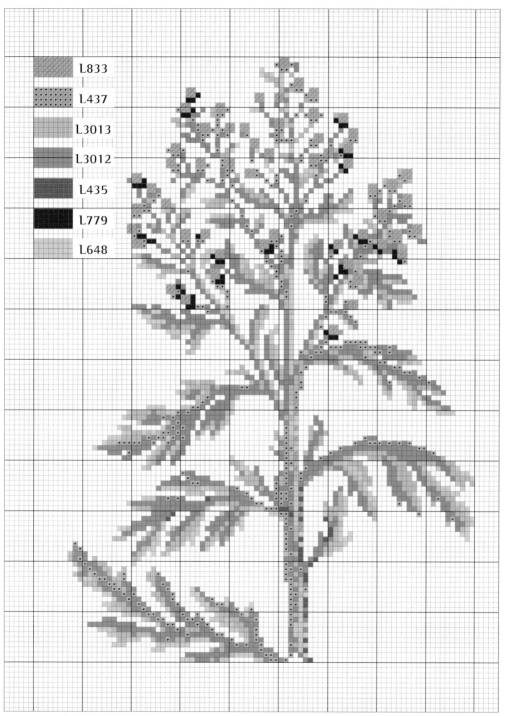

	L833
	L437
	L3013
	L3012
	L435
	L779
	L648

Wormwood/Artemisia absinthium

Linen DMC 842

Medicinal plants

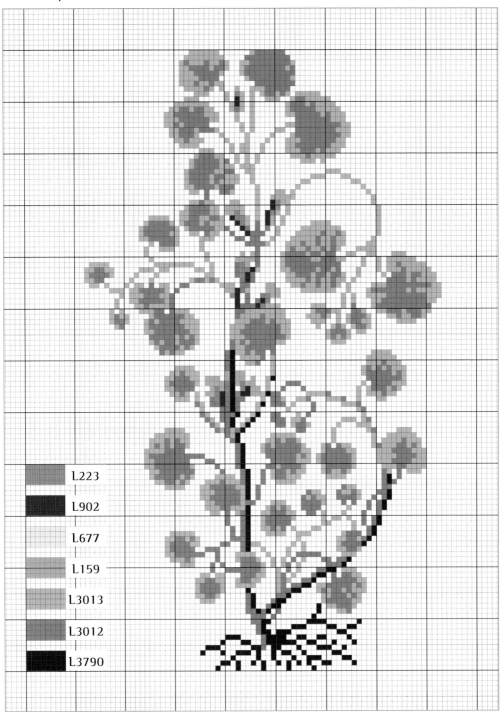

L223
L902
L677
L159
L3013
L3012
L3790

Ground ivy/Glechoma hederacea L.

Linen DMC 762

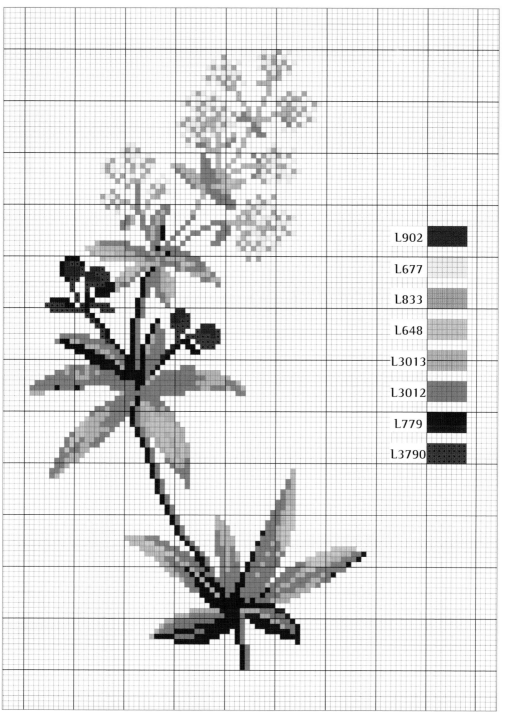

Madder/Rubia tinctorum L.

Linen DMC 3865

L902	
L677	
L833	
L648	
L3013	
L3012	
L779	
L3790	

Medicinal plants

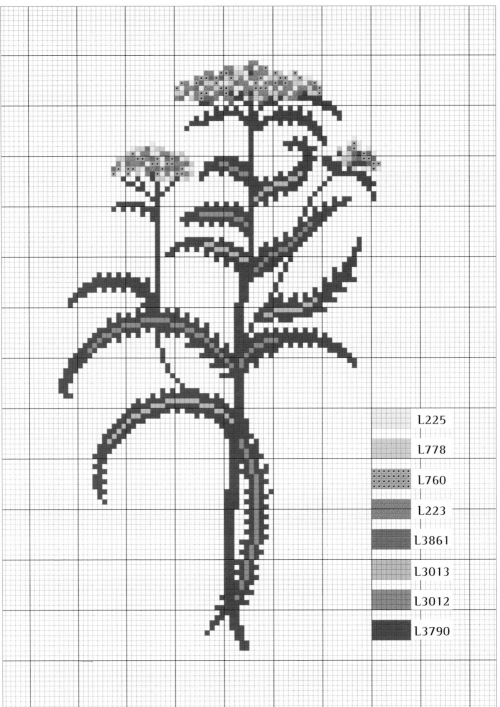

L225
L778
L760
L223
L3861
L3013
L3012
L3790

Yarrow/Achillea millefolium   Linen DMC 3865

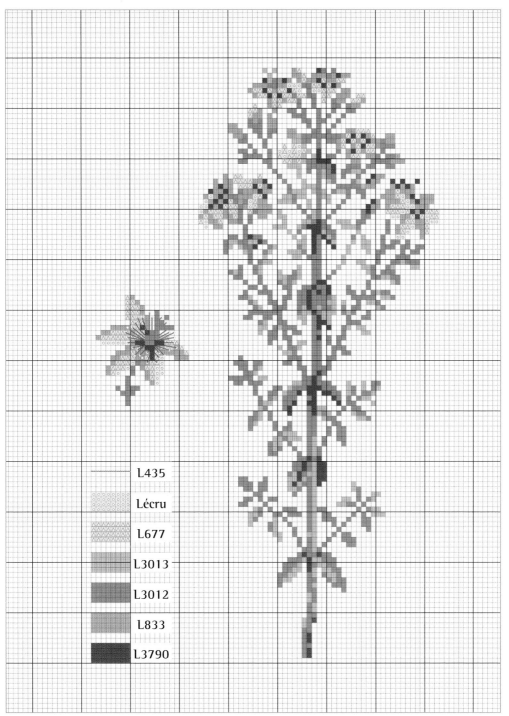

L435
Lécru
L677
L3013
L3012
L833
L3790

St John's wort/Hypericum perforatum L.

Linen DMC 712

Edible seaside plants

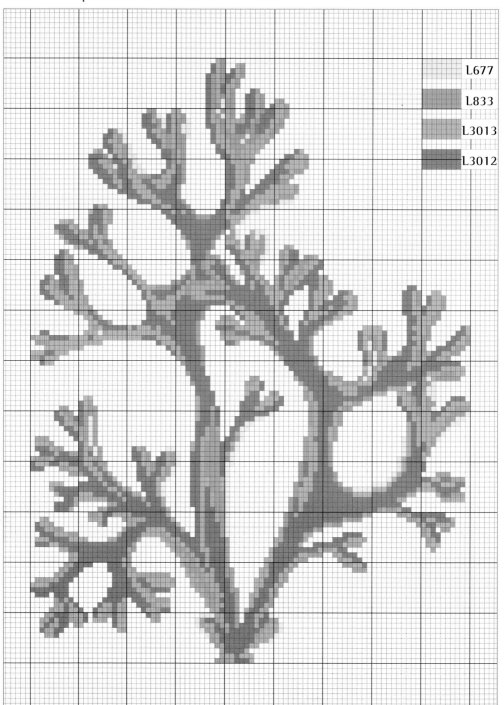

L677
L833
L3013
L3012

Seaweed/Fucus L.

Linen DMC 712

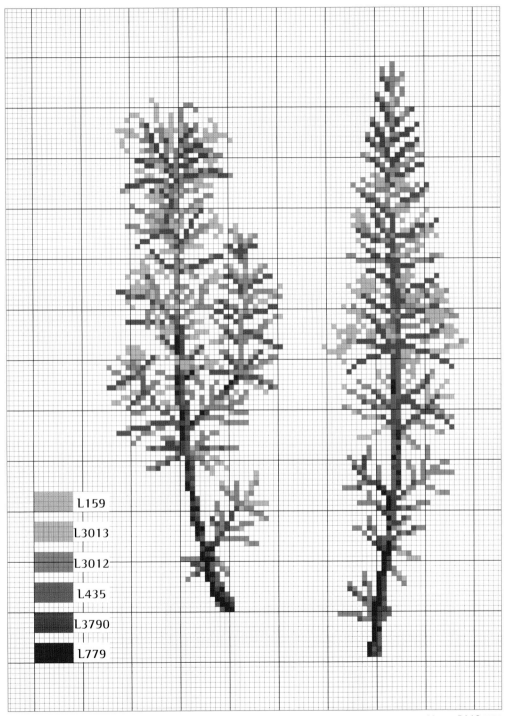

L159
L3013
L3012
L435
L3790
L779

Rosemary/Rosmarinus officinalis L.

Linen DMC 762

Edible seaside plants

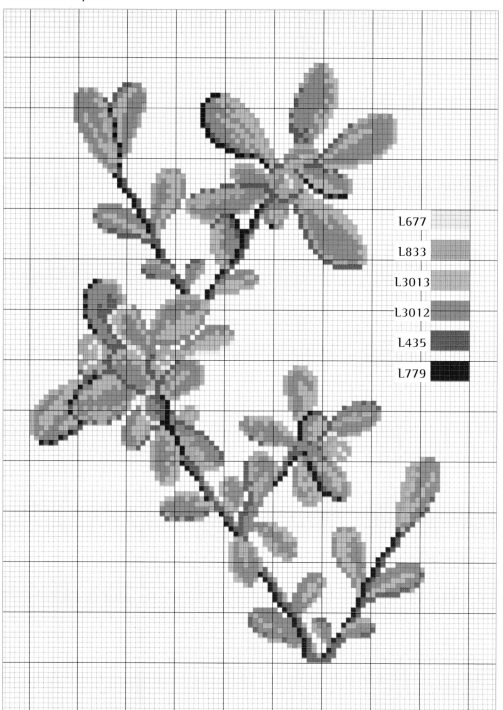

L677
L833
L3013
L3012
L435
L779

Purslane/Portulaca oleracea

Linen DMC 712

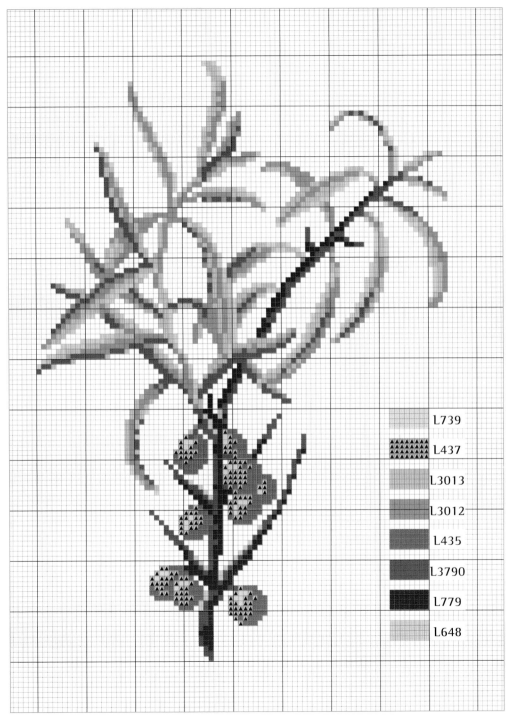

L739

L437

L3013

L3012

L435

L3790

L779

L648

Sea buckthorn/Hippophae rhamnoides   Linen DMC 3840

Edible meadow plants

	L225
▲▲▲	L967
	L760
	L223
	L902
	Lécru
	L437
	L3013
	L3012
	L3790

Daisy/Bellis perennis L.

Linen DMC 3743

L677
L833
L3013
L3012
L435
L779
L3790
L648

Cowslip/Primula veris L.

Linen DMC 3743

Edible meadow plants

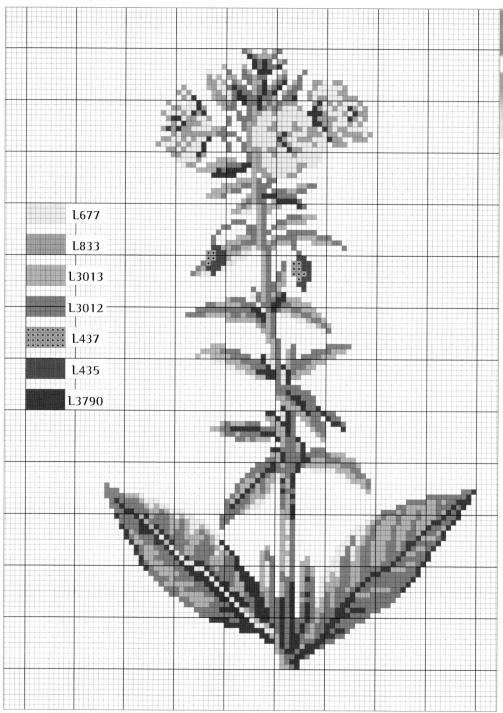

L677
L833
L3013
L3012
L437
L435
L3790

Evening primrose/Oenothera biennis L.

Linen DMC 772

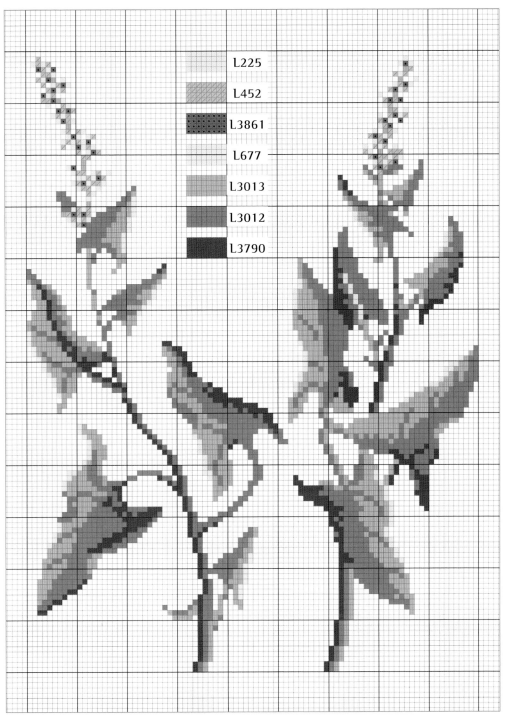

Good King Henry/Chenopodium Bonus-Henricus L.

Linen DMC 225

Legend:
- L225
- L452
- L3861
- L677
- L3013
- L3012
- L3790

Edible meadow plants

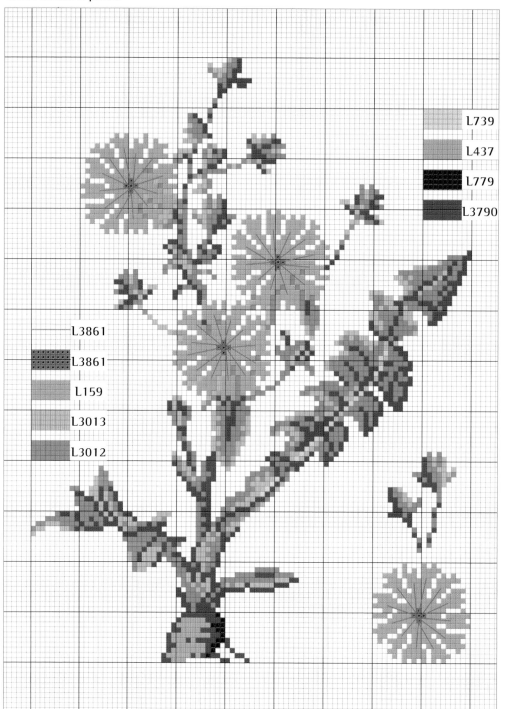

L739
L437
L779
L3790

L3861
L3861
L159
L3013
L3012

Chicory/Cichorium intybus L.

Linen DMC 3866

Legend:
- L677
- L3013
- L3012
- L435
- L3790

Stinging nettle/Urtica dioica

Linen DMC 3782

Edible scrubland plants

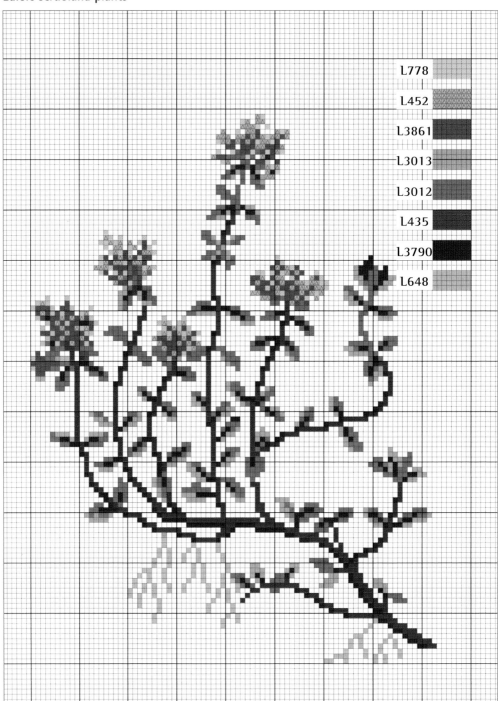

L778
L452
L3861
L3013
L3012
L435
L3790
L648

Thyme/Thymus vulgaris L.

Linen DMC 3866

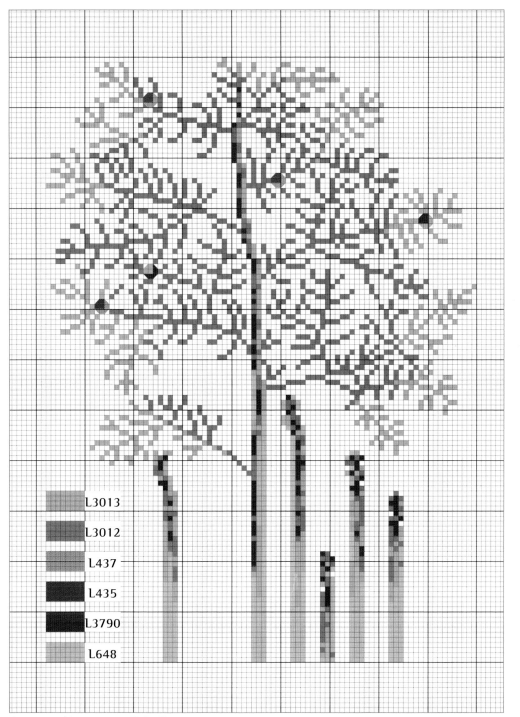

L3013

L3012

L437

L435

L3790

L648

Asparagus/Asparagus officinalis   Linen DMC 842

Edible scrubland plants

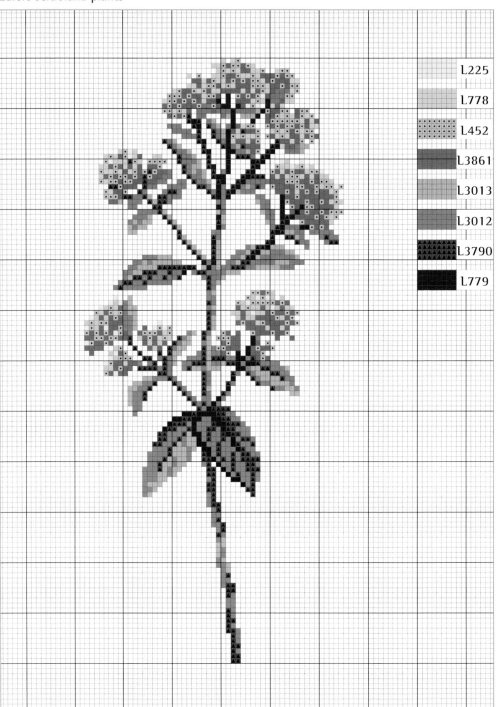

	L225
	L778
	L452
	L3861
	L3013
	L3012
	L3790
	L779

Oregano/Origanum vulgare L.

Linen DMC 3866

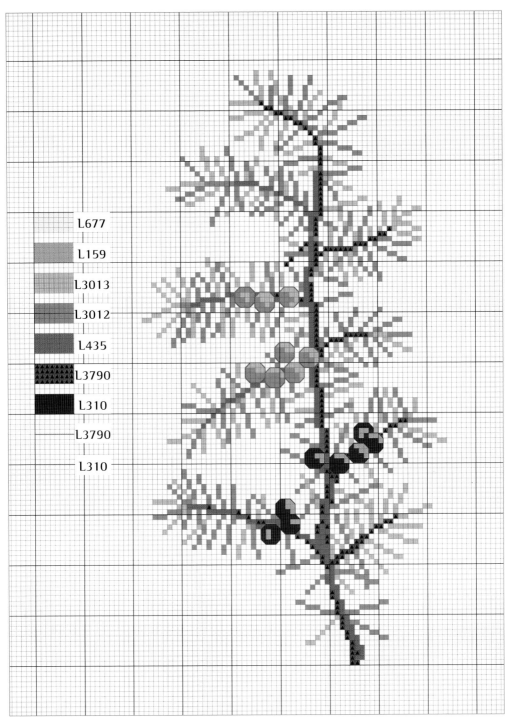

L677
L159
L3013
L3012
L435
L3790
L310
L3790
L310

Juniper/Juniperus communis

Linen DMC 712

Little garden fruits

L760
L223
L902
L677

L3013
L3012

L833
L3790
L779

Fig/Ficus carica

Linen DMC 3823

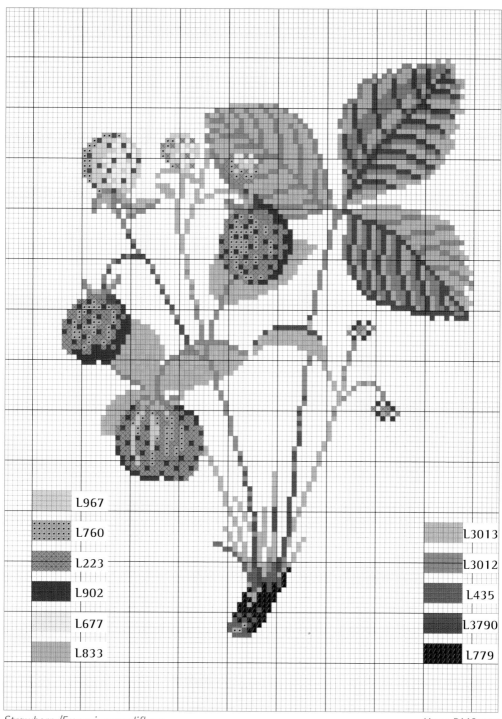

L967
L760
L223
L902
L677
L833

L3013
L3012
L435
L3790
L779

Strawberry/Fragaria grandiflora

Linen DMC 772

Little garden fruits

L760
L223
L902
L739
L833
L3013
L3012
L779
L3790
L648

Cherry/Prunus

Linen DMC 225

L225
L452
L778
L223
L902

L3013
L3012
L437
L435
L3790
L779

Grape vine/Vitis vinifera L.

Linen DMC 225

Edible flowers

L778
L760
L223
L3013
L3012
L3790
L822
L648

Cotton thistle/Onopordum acanthium   Linen DMC 772

L437

L225

L223

L902

L677

L437

L3013

L3012

L779

Dog rose/Rosa canina L.

Linen DMC 712

Edible flowers

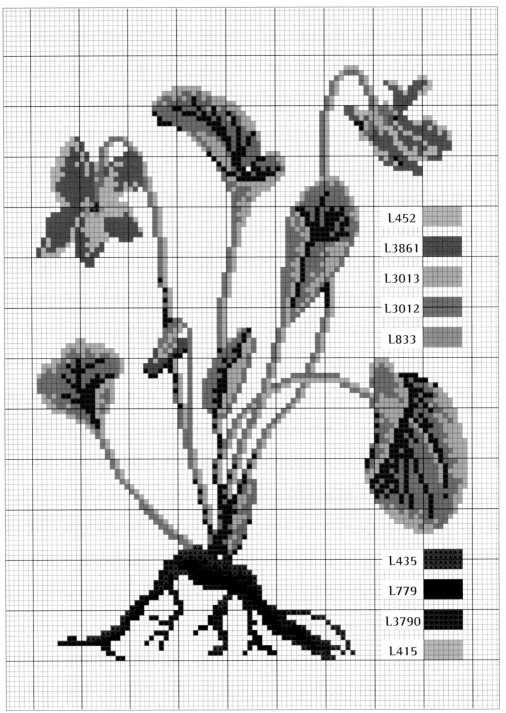

L452
L3861
L3013
L3012
L833

L435
L779
L3790
L415

Violet/Viola

Linen DMC 3865

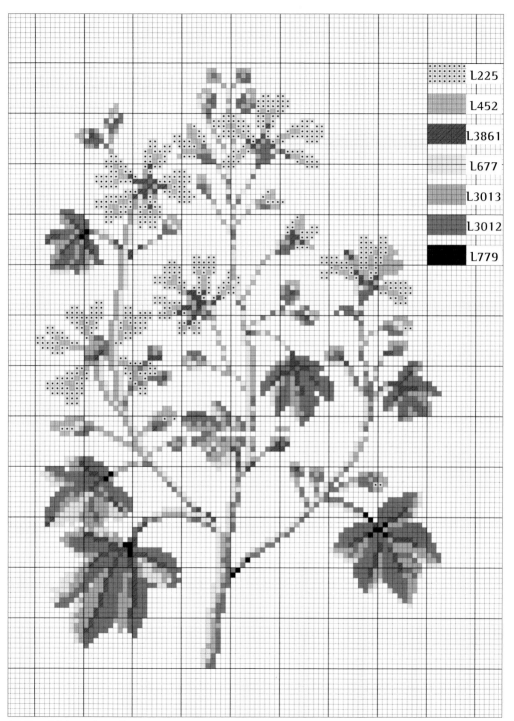

Mallow/Malva sylvestris

Linen DMC 3865

Legend:
- L225
- L452
- L3861
- L677
- L3013
- L3012
- L779

Edible flowers

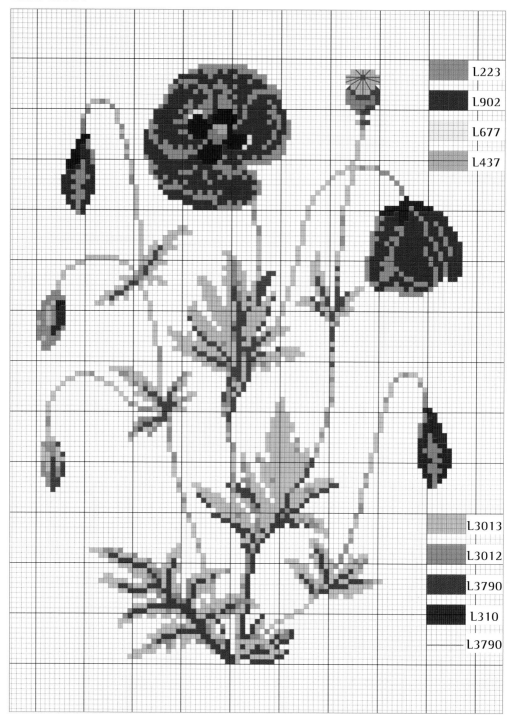

	L223
	L902
	L677
	L437

	L3013
	L3012
	L3790
	L310
	L3790

Poppy/Papaver rhoeas L.

Linen DMC 3743

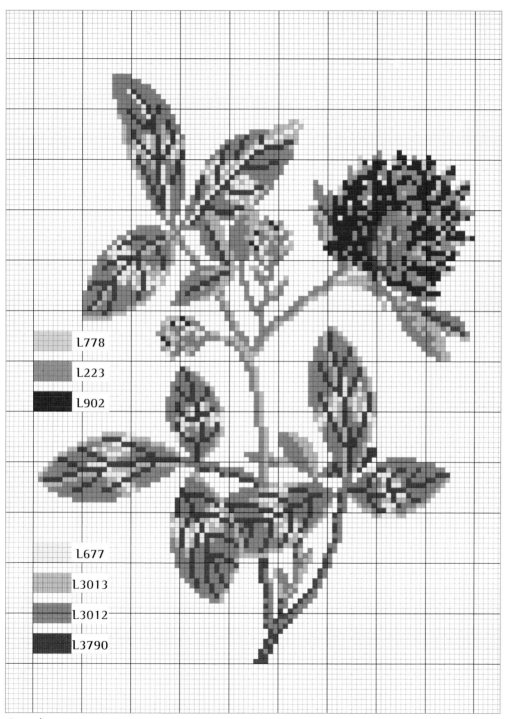

L778
L223
L902

L677
L3013
L3012
L3790

Clover/Trifolium

Linen DMC 3743

technical tips

A fun and easy technique

Cross stitch will help you create beautiful pieces of embroidery, and it is deceptively simple to achieve. It is actually one of the easiest stitches – all you need to know is how to count! In the past it was customary for young girls to learn cross stitch, and history has left us with a number of exquisite samplers made by the agile, small hands of these girls. If, like them, you decide to take the plunge, you will see how easily you can achieve remarkable results and how enjoyable cross stitching can be.

The design

Cross stitch embroidery is carried out according to a design on a squared, coloured grid, which forms the pattern. Each square of colour corresponds to a stitch to be embroidered on the fabric. Sometimes the pattern is in black and white and, in this case, different symbols are used for each colour. The same symbol always corresponds to the same colour throughout the piece. Squares with no colour or without a symbol indicate that no stitch is required.

If you are a cross stitch beginner, use a fabric known as aida rather than DMC cotton or linen even-weave fabrics. Aida has the advantage of a coarser weft, which closely resembles the squares in the pattern. More experienced stitchers who work on even-weaves will convert each square of the grid on to the fabric by stitching over a group of threads, the number of which will always be identical, both in height and width.

Cross stitch

Cross stitch is elementary both in appearance and in execution. Quite simply, it is made up of two inter-laced diagonal stitches. It can be stitched on its own or continuously. In this case, in order to ensure a beautiful finish, it is important to always stitch the crosses in the same direction, from bottom left to top right; then, on the way back, from bottom right to top left.

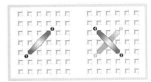

Simple cross stitch

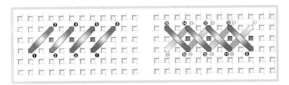

Continuous cross stitch

If you stitch on an even-weave fabric or over one fabric thread, always complete one stitch before moving on to the next. This will ensure that your work is even.

Important comment

Never make a knot when you start a thread, as it will be seen when the cross stitch is complete and has been ironed. To start a thread length, use your finger to keep hold of a short piece of the thread on the reverse of your work, and work over it with the first stitches to hold it in place.
To end a thread, turn over your work, slip your thread under the last three or four stitches and cut the thread.

Combining stitches with cross stitch

Some embroidery stitches can be combined with cross stitch to create a look that cross stitch alone cannot achieve, for example to underline a shape.

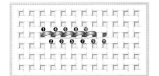

Half cross stitch or tapestry stitch

You can use half cross stitch, also known as tapestry stitch, to create shadows on the background and soften the colour intensity.

Three-quarter cross stitch allows you to make the edges of a design more precise and is often bordered by a top stitch. This stitch allows you to avoid 'steps' in the sense that the return movement of the thread closes the stitch, either by the right or by the left.

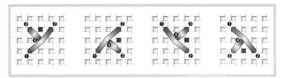

Three-quarter cross stitch

Top stitch

Top stitch is ideal for shaping the design and accentuating it, just as a pencil line would do. It is stitched when the entire cross stitch design is complete. It is done using fewer threads than cross stitch and more often with a colour in a darker tone.

Finally, use a quarter cross stitch to create fine detail. It is used mainly on an even-weave on a single fabric thread.

Tip

If the strands of your thread length become twisted, turn your work over and let your needle hang down loose. The thread will unravel automatically and return to the correct position.

Satin stitch is found on work embroidered on both aida and even-weave fabrics. It creates a smooth, solid area of colour or an outline.

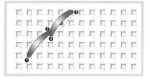

Satin stitch

Preparing the fabric

Before embroidering with cross stitch, you need to prepare the fabric by whipping the edges. This prevents the edges of the fabric from fraying. You could instead apply an adhesive ribbon along the edges of the fabric. The piece of fabric must be a little larger than your embroidery pattern so it can be framed when it is complete.

Fold your fabric into four to find the centre, then tack two rows, one horizontal, the other vertical along the folds. These rows of tacking stitch provide a reference point for stitching and will be removed once the cross stitch is finished. The centre of the design is indicated on the pattern by small arrows located on the sides of the grid. To find the centre of the design, follow the horizontal and vertical axes with your finger, using the arrows.

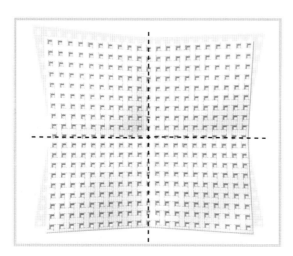

Do not leave long threads at the back of your work. If the stitches in the same colour are approximately 2cm (¾in) apart, you can slip your thread and continue embroidering. If the stitches are further apart (more than 2cm (¾in)), pass the thread under the other stitches, cut, and start again with a new piece of thread.

Finishing

When your cross stitch design is complete, remove the two rows of tacking. Wash the cross stitched fabric gently in cold water and, once dry, iron on the reverse using a damp cloth to protect the fabric.

Framing

Allow at least 7cm (2¾in) around the edges of your work to frame it. Cut a piece of strong cardboard a little smaller than your frame. Place you work on a table, wrong side facing up, and put the cardboard over the top, centring it over the design. Using a strong, thick thread, lace together the upper and lower edges of the work. Be careful not to damage the piece, and tighten the thread regularly to keep the fabric taut. Lace the other two sides together in the same way. Place the laced work in the frame under the glass, and it is finished.

Accessories

Needle

The needle used for cross stitch is a round-ended needle with a wider eye than a sewing needle. Its rounded end does not damage the weft; the size of the eye allows several strands to be threaded through. A No. 26 needle is suitable for working with a single strand, but you will need a No. 24 needle to work with two or three strands. The size of the needle varies according to the weft. Embroidery needles are available to buy in packets of mixed sizes or one size.

Tip

To give relief to your work, you can also place a piece of quilting between the cardboard and the fabric. In this case, your work will not be framed under glass but will be enhanced by the frame you choose. You can also hang your stitched picture using small lengths of wooden beading placed at the top and bottom.

Embroiderers' hoop

Sometimes it is necessary to use a hoop, especially when working on an even-weave or very flexible fabric. It allows you to stretch the fabric and keep the stitches even. Embroiderers' hoops can be fixed on to a table, but we recommend hoops that are easier to carry around with you.

Scissors

Small pointed scissors are best, and use them only for your embroidery. Decorative scissors are available, for example in the shape of a bird, as well as other novelty items for you to hang on the handles so they are easier to find. When you travel, make sure that you keep your scissors separate from your fabric to avoid accidentally cutting your embroidery.

Magnetic board and magnifying rule

Fixing the pattern for your work to a magnetic board allows you to follow the line of your design more easily. The magnifying rule helps you follow the design easily and magnifies it at the same time, which is easier on your eyes.

Boxes for storing threads

You could buy an organiser to keep your threads in. These are cardboard boxes with perforations near the edges which allow you to tidy away your threads and note the reference numbers in the margin.

You could darn your threads on to darning wool boxes and keep each coloured thread in a new box.

Finally, you could use plastic wallets to organise your prepared cardboard sections.

Tip

A needle threader is handy when you need to thread two or three strands together for a single thread length.

Tip

Move the hoop regularly and protect the edges with tissue paper so you don't damage the fabric.

Tip

A thimble will protect your middle finger. If you become a lover of cross stitch you will be forever picking up your work whenever and wherever you can, and you'll be grateful for a thimble!

Tip

Keep a record of the threads you use. This will be useful if you run out of a colour or wish to create the same design again.

Classic fabrics
DMC aida

Aida is easy to use as the threads form regular squares. It is available in different sizes: 3 stitches, 4 stitches, 5.5 stitches and 7 stitches per centimetre.

The size of your work will depend on the fabric you choose. The fewer stitches the fabric has, per centimetre, the larger the finished work will be. For example, embroidery on a 3-stitches per centimetre aida will be much bigger than embroidery on a 7-stitches per centimetre aida.

The table below shows the approximate length of the fabric, in centimetres, for ten stitches. If you already have an idea of the size of your project, these conversion references might be useful.

Aida fabric	Length for ten stitches	Number of strands to use
3 stitches/cm	3.1cm (1¼in)	Three or four
4 stitches/cm	2.5cm (1in)	Three
5.5 stitches/cm	1.81cm (¾in)	Two or three
7 stitches/cm	1.4cm (½in)	One or two

DMC even-weave and linen fabric

Using linen or cotton allows you to choose the size of your cross stitches. They are a little more difficult to use than aida as they are not woven in squares but this difficulty is largely offset by a more refined result.

Stitching over two

The table below shows the expected sizes if you stitch each cross over two fabric threads in height and width.

Linen fabrics	Length for ten stitches	Number of strands to use
8 count [8 threads/cm]	2.5cm (1in)	Three or four
10 count	2cm (¾in)	Two or three
11 count	1.82cm (½in)	Two or three
12 count	1.66cm (½in)	One or two
14 count	1.4cm (½in)	One

Even-weave	Length for ten stitches	Number of strands to use
10 threads/cm	2cm (¾in)	Two or three

Tip

All these fabrics exist in numerous colours, either by the metre or as remnants. Do not hesitate to ask your haberdasher for advice.

Stitching over one

The table below shows the expected sizes if you stitch each cross over one fabric thread in height and width.

Linen fabrics	Length for ten stitches	Number of strands to use
8 count	1.25cm (½in)	One
10 count	1cm (½in)	One
11 count	0.9cm (½in)	One
12 count	0.83cm (½in)	One

Cotton even-weave	Length for ten stitches	Number of strands to use
10 count	1cm (½in)	One

Tip

If you are stitching on dark fabric, place a pale cloth over your knees to help you see more easily where to insert your needle.

Pre-cut fabrics

DMC aida, linen fabric or even-weave are available in a variety of colours, either by the metre or as remnants. These pre-cut fabrics are available in two sizes:
35 × 47cm (14 × 18½in) and
50 × 78cm (19½ × 30½in).

Dream fabrics

Do you want to embroider a tablecloth, a bath towel or a bib? Do you want to decorate a pretty tea towel with designs? There are numerous products available to allow you to do so, and you will find many kits in shops to satisfy your growing passion.

Let's imagine that your fabric is 10 count and your design is 52 stitches over 52. If you work over two fabric threads, this is 10÷2 = 5 stitches/cm, and your work will therefore be 52÷5 = 10.4cm (4in). If you work over three fabric threads, this is 10÷3 = 3.33 stitches/cm, and your work will be 52÷3.33 = 15.62cm (6in).

These values are approximate as they depend on how tightly you stitch.

Vinyl or carded fabrics

These are often used for small embroidered items, such as bookmarks or to make mobiles or birthday cake decorations. Stitch the chosen design and cut out, either around the edge of the design or in the shape of the finished item (for example, an extended rectangle for a bookmark).

Pulled-thread fabric

This even-weave fabric is designed specifically for pulled thread work and allows you to stitch on any background fabric. Use a hoop to hold the work in place, then stitch the design using the pulled-thread fabric fixed to the surface of your chosen background fabric.

Cross stitches are made through the two thicknesses of fabric. When the design is complete, pull the threads of the pulled-thread fabric one by one using tweezers. The cross stitches will remain on the background fabric.

Tip

To find out the number of threads per centimetre of a fabric you want to turn into a table-cloth for example, place two pins 1cm (½in) apart and count the threads between them.

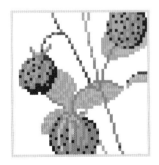

Canvas

Canvas is a fairly stiff fabric and is available in several weights. It is usually made of cotton or linen and varies in the tightness of the weave. It is ideal for making cushions and chair or sofa covers, but you can also use it as a pulled-thread fabric. Simply dampen your work and, using tweezers, pull the threads of the canvas one by one.

Threads

DMC Mouliné stranded cotton

Mouliné stranded cotton thread has a shiny appearance and is available in about 460 colours. Mouliné stranded cotton is the thread most often used for cross stitch. It has six strands that are easily separated. Available in variegated shades, these produce a wonderful effect in your finished embroidery but demand no more effort from the stitcher than a plain stranded cotton thread.

DMC metallic Mouliné stranded cotton

This thread is presented in two ways: in the form of either a six-strand skein or a three-strand bobbin. Sixteen colours are available, including bicoloured and multicoloured threads.

Tip

If you work with variegated Mouliné stranded cotton, complete one stitch at a time before moving on to the next so there isn't too much of a difference in tone between the thread lengths. When you begin a new thread length, take care to start with the same tone. If you finish with a light tone, start again with a light tone and similarly with a dark tone.

You can also mix a strand of metallic Mouliné stranded cotton with a strand of traditional Mouliné stranded cotton in very close colours to produce a different effect. Experiment by replacing traditional Mouliné stranded cotton with metallic Mouliné stranded cotton. Your work will take on a completely different appearance!

The table below will help you find the traditional Mouliné stranded cotton and the corresponding metallic Mouliné stranded cotton.

Metallics	5272	5289	5288	5291	5290	5287
Traditional Mouliné stranded cotton	5200	208	316	798	806	413
Metallics	5282	5283	5284	5279	5270	5269
Traditional Mouliné stranded cotton	834	762	833	3064	816	3818

DMC matt-folded thread

This non-divisible thread is suitable for use with thick cotton fabrics.

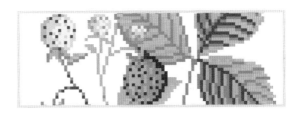

Pearl cotton No. 3, No. 5 and No. 8

Pearl cotton is available in skeins or balls and has a satin appearance. There are 292 shades of pearl cotton No. 3, 312 shades of No. 5 and 238 shades of No. 8.

This shiny looking thread, which considerably enhances stitching work, is used on thick fabrics, for example to embroider tablecloths, place mats and other table linen.

Multicoloured pearl cotton

Multicoloured pearl cotton, also known as Castelbajac thread, varies gradually from one colour to the next along its length. It should be stitched using the same technique as the variegated Mouliné stranded cotton, on a thick fabric, as this thread is a pearl cotton No. 8.

Medicis wool

You can also use wool for your cross stitch work. When used on linen, Medicis wool gives an antique appearance. It is available in 178 colours.

Creative ideas

Tip for adventurous stitchers

You can add more depth and style to your work by mixing the threads. Mixing threads is fun, and creates unique and sometimes surprising results. To add subtle shading, mix a strand of light coloured Mouliné stranded cotton with a strand of darker Mouliné stranded cotton in the same tonal range.

Experiment with the number of thread strands according to your fabric; the more strands you stitch with, the denser the colour. You can create more delicate and light embroidery using fewer strands.

If you have a design of your own that you'd like to embroider in cross stitch, you first need to convert it into a cross stitch pattern using transparent, squared paper. You can find this in haberdashery shops, and it is specially designed for this purpose.

It is best to choose a simple design as too much detail can ruin the work. Place the squared paper over the design and trace the outline with a pencil. To make a cross stitch pattern, change the shapes by adapting each line to a series of squares.

When drawing your pattern, if your pencil line is in the centre or in the upper part of a square, colour the square above; but colour the square below if the pencil line is in the lower part of the square. Colour the squares on your pattern with coloured pencils to match the design you are copying. You are now ready to stitch your own creation!

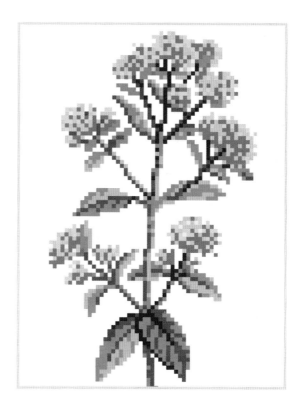

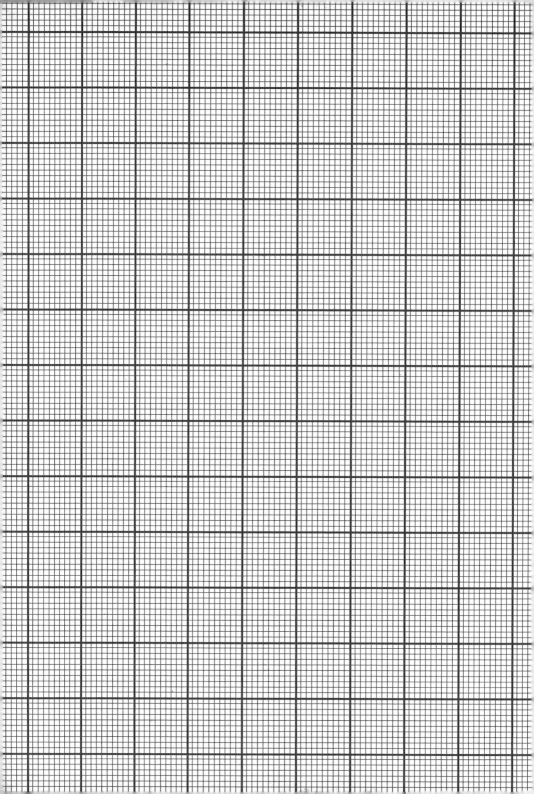